Rachel Worth is Course Director for B.A. (Hons) Fashion Studies at the Arts Institute at Bournemouth, and lives in Swanage. She read history at Cambridge, and did her MA in the history of dress at the Courtauld Institute of Art, London. She is a well-known authority on the history of rural working-class dress, about which she has frequently lectured and been widely published.

Following page
Dorset character Dickie Burgess wearing a traditional hat
and coat-style smock-frock, in about 1920.
His clothes are old-fashioned for this date, the smock-frock
having passed out of general fashion by the 1880s. However,
older people tended to continue to wear the styles of their

DISCOVER DORSET

DRESS AND TEXTILES

RACHEL WORTH

A cottager in a sun-bonnet fetching water in
Stoke Abbot in 1900. Since 1953 the water has
been fed through a lion's head, put there to
celebrate the Coronation.

First published in 2002 by The Dovecote Press Ltd
Stanbridge, Wimborne, Dorset BH21 4JD

ISBN 1 874336 98 9

Series designed by Humphrey Stone

Typeset in Monotype Sabon
Printed and bound by Baskerville Press, Salisbury, Wiltshire

A CIP catalogue record for this book is available
from the British Library

CONTENTS

INTRODUCTION

The principal manufactures are those of flax and hemp, chiefly carried on in the neighbourhood of Bridport and Beaminster; at Shaftesbury, shirt buttons and coarse woollen cloths; at Blandford, shirt buttons; at Stalbridge and Sherborne silk is spun, and at Wimborne many women and children are employed in knitting worsted stockings. At Poole and Abbotsbury, some plain and striped cottons are wove; and at the latter place, sail-cloth, sacking, cables, ropes, large nets and cod-lines for the Newfoundland fishery, and mackerel nets for home use are made. Beaminster participates in the manufacture of sail-cloth and many individuals in the country around find employment in spinning the flax and preparing the materials. Taken altogether, this county holds not by any means an eminent situation as a manufacturing one; agriculture, its fisheries and stone quarries are the main contributors to the prosperity of Dorsetshire (*Pigot's Trade Directory of Dorsetshire*, 1830).

Someone visiting Dorset on holiday would perhaps be incredulous to hear it being described as an 'industrial' county, either now or in the past. Certainly there is little evidence for such a claim in the tourist brochures. It may then come as a surprise to read in *Pigot's Trade Directory for Dorsetshire* an entry for Blandford in 1823 which states that 'the principal support of the town and neighbouring villages, is the manufacture of thread, waistcoat and shirt buttons, which employs several hundred women and children'. In the same directory, Sherborne was described as 'formerly the most frequented town in the county, for its manufactories of woollen cloths, shirt buttons,

By 1892, when this photograph was taken, the cotton sun-bonnet and apron being worn by this cottager in Upwey were being replaced by cheaper ready-to-wear clothing, bringing to an end the wearing of Dorset's traditional rural clothing.

haberdashery wares and bone lace', and 'still gives employment to several hundred hands in the manufacture or spinning of silk, all the other manufactures having ceased'.

Dorset remains, primarily, a rural county, its main 'industry' being concerned with farming, but it is important not to forget the numerous local industries, some of which existed up until the end of the nineteenth century. Before the widespread availability of cheap ready-made clothing towards the end of the nineteenth century, people either made their clothes themselves or, if well off enough to afford it, had them made by tailors and dressmakers. Therefore, it is not surprising that, as in other rural counties, a large number of working people's lives were intimately associated with the production of textiles and clothing. While some industries such as the silk industry were conducted in factories, others such as 'gloving' and 'buttony' relied primarily on the handicraft skills of women and children working at home.

Lists of the goods which made up the cargoes of ships leaving Dorset ports for Newfoundland's salted cod trade in the seventeenth and eighteenth centuries provide a fascinating insight into, among other goods, the variety of clothing and textiles being produced at the time. A typical cargo was carried by the ship *Roberta,* which left Weymouth in February 1682. This included *linen*, soap, rugs and fishing lines. The *Willing Mind* left Poole in April 1709 carrying *made-up garments*, malt, flour, sail-cloth, nails, cordage, rugs, *woollen cloth, serges, shoes*, blankets, nets and lines. Seven Poole vessels cleared port in 1755 carrying a total of 1,825 *made garments*, in addition to *cloth, hats, gloves, shirts, stockings and shoes*. A substantial proportion of these cargoes are likely to have been produced in Dorset and were intended for the maintenance of the Newfoundland trade and the upkeep of the crew, as well as for the 'passengers' who annually crossed the Atlantic to seek work in the fishing trade, and the farmers who chose to remain on the island during the winter.

The production of woollen cloth, linen and silk for clothing; the making of essential accessories such as gloves, stockings and dressmaking aids such as haberdashery (ribbons, lace and buttons) occupied thousands of men, women and children for many centuries.

Every town and village of substantial size had its share of dressmakers and shoemakers. Where possible, industries such as the famous Dorset 'buttony' were conducted alongside agricultural occupations, by workers who were pleased to be able to work at home on goods for commercial consumption well into the nineteenth century. The uncertainties of a livelihood dependent purely on the vagaries of the agricultural calendar meant that, not infrequently, families needed to find ways of supplementing meagre earnings, which was possible until these crafts were mechanised in the mid-nineteenth century. The silk-spinning industries of Gillingham and Sherborne, however, were mechanised in the mid-eighteenth century. For the most part, workers in these towns had to work in mills and could not, therefore, combine their craft with agricultural occupations.

The history of the development and subsequent decline of those industries in Dorset associated with the provision of clothing and textiles is the subject of this book. In one sense, then, it is an economic history of the county. On another level, however, it is very much a social history concerned both with the people who made these items, as well as with those for whom they were made. Unmistakable and unique Dorset 'knob' buttons; elaborately embroidered smock-frocks; brightly-coloured striped silk ribbons still survive in a number of Dorset museums and bear witness to the enormous amount of time and effort expended in order to eke out a living or, in the case of a smock-frock, to make an essential item of clothing for a loved one.

TEXTILE INDUSTRIES

WOOLLEN CLOTH

One of the oldest textile industries is that of woollen cloth. In the days before the widespread availability of cotton, let alone the development of man-made and synthetic fabrics in the twentieth century, the majority of the population's clothing was most likely to be made either from wool, linen or hemp, or a mixture of linen and wool known as *linsey-wolsey,* while silk was generally confined to the wealthy upper classes.

Dorset, with its extensive areas of chalk downland, ideal for the grazing of sheep, marked the eastern extent of the great woollen cloth industry which developed in the south-west of England during the Middle Ages and which was concentrated in Gloucestershire, Somerset and Wiltshire. Although never as extensive or as profitable as the Wiltshire woollen cloth industry, even in 1823 the industry in Dorset was described as 'considerable', albeit much declined since the days of its former glory. According to the *Victoria County History,* cloth was made at Sturminster Newton until 1820.

The Dorset woollen industry specialised in both the production of the raw material as well as in the processing of fabric. Wool obtained from the traditional Dorset Horn breed of sheep and later, the Dorset Down breed (the latter developed in the mid-nineteenth century) is of a particularly fine texture and has a short staple, suitable for both the hosiery trade and for fine knitting yarns as well as for woven cloth.

There is little information about the woollen cloth industry in medieval times. Indeed, Dorset was not famous for the quality of its wool during this period. However, it must have been sufficiently important for a wool staple to have been established in 1364 at Melcombe Regis during the reign of Edward I. (This privilege was later taken away by Henry VI, who bestowed it upon Poole.) The high cost of export of woollen cloth via the staple at Calais led to

A team of sheep-shearers at work at Chilcombe in about 1880.

evasion of customs duty in a number of cases. There were other kinds of problems reported too: in 1389 there were complaints that substandard cloth was being sold in Dorset, Somerset and Gloucestershire. The merchant buyers were being duped by being sold cloth which was folded in such a way as to disguise damaged areas of cloth inside. The merchants were exporting the cloth overseas and there were cases in which they were 'at death's door, and imprisoned and put to fine and ransom by the foreigners on account of the cloth'.

In the fourteenth century the great Dorset estates began to concentrate on the increasingly profitable sheep flocks to satisfy the rising demand both at home and abroad for West Country wool and cloth. As J.H. Bettey has pointed out in his book *Farming* (also in this series), it was during the fifteenth century that the huge sheep flocks – which were to become a distinctive characteristic of Dorset farming – were assembled. For example, by 1535, the Dorset monastery of Milton possessed over 7000 sheep, while Cerne had over 6000. Sheep-farming in Dorset was intimately connected with the requirements of the woollen industry. The principal purpose of the development and management of water-meadows bordering on the quick-flowing streams in the area round Whitchurch Canonicorum in

Sheep-shearing at Bradford Peverell in about 1885. This skilled job was
traditionally the preserve of men, although in this photograph a woman in
a sun-bonnet helps, just like Maryann in Thomas Hardy's *Far From the
Madding Crowd*, who 'throws the loose locks into the middle of the fleece,
rolls it up, and carries it into the battleground as three-and-a-half pounds
of unadulterated warmth...'.

West Dorset, for example, was to provide an early bite for ewes and
lambs.

Like Gabriel Oak in Thomas Hardy's novel *Far from the Madding
Crowd* (first published in 1874), the shepherd was a respected and
indispensable figure in the life of the countryside. Equally, the
shearing of sheep was a highly skilled job and an important event in
the farming calendar. The annual sheep-shearing ritual is vividly
described in Hardy's novel: it takes place in early June on Bathsheba
Everdene's farm in the great barn (or shearing-barn) in Hardy's
Weatherbury (Puddletown). Hardy describes how, after the shearing
Maryann comes to take the wool away:

'Then up comes Maryann; throws the loose locks into the middle of the
fleece, rolls it up, and carries it into the battleground as three-and-a-half
pounds of unadulterated warmth for the winter enjoyment of persons
unknown and far away, who will, however, never experience the

Built in the 1590s, Louds Mill, near Dorchester, was an important
fulling mill. During the fulling process, the woven cloth was
shrunk or felted and cleaned by placing it in a vat with a mixture
of Fuller's Earth and urine where it was pounded by wooden
fulling stocks. Louds Mill later became a corn mill, but only a
fragment of one wall still stands.

superlative comfort derivable from the wool as it here exists, new and pure
– before the unctuousness of its nature whilst in a living state has dried,
stiffened, and been washed out – rendering it just now as superior to
anything woollen as cream is superior to milk-and-water.'

Interestingly, Hardy contrasts the beauty and purity of the newly
shorn wool with the manufactured wool which is subsequently made
into a garment. This was a complex process. After spinning and
weaving, the wool was fulled. Woven cloth was shrunk or felted and
cleaned by being placed in a vat with a mixture of Fuller's Earth and
urine where it was pounded by wooden fulling stocks (similar to large
hammers) operated by a water wheel. The earliest reference in Dorset
to a fulling mill for the treatment of woollen cloth appears to have
been at East and West Stour in 1300. By this time, a number of fulling
mills (also known as 'tucking mills') had been established in the West
Country, often alongside existing corn mills or even in the same

building. Other mills used at one time for fulling woollen cloth include Walford Mill (Wimborne), which is recorded as being a fulling mill in 1552 and 1591, and one at Stour Provost. Louds Mill, near Dorchester, was built in the 1590s for fulling and an early seventeenth century map shows tentering racks nearby (used for stretching, drying and bleaching the cloth). There were also fulling mills at Bridport, Cerne Abbas, Lyme Regis and Wareham (Carey Farm), which chart the expansion of the woollen cloth industry.

The introduction of woad in the late sixteenth century reflected the general move on the part of innovative farmers to introduce new and profitable crops. Previously imported (from France, Germany, the Low Countries and Spain), the leaves of the woad plant produced a rich blue dye, which also formed the basis of all blacks, greens and other dark colours used in the woollen cloth industry. It was soon grown extensively in West Dorset and in the area around Cranborne. In 1585 a government enquiry found that a total of 657 acres of woad was being grown in Dorset, much of it on the chalklands of the north-eastern part of the county. Salisbury clothiers, who were in great need of the dye, leased land specifically for the cultivation of woad: for example, in 1599, one George Bedford joined with another Salisbury clothier, Robert Eyre, to lease sixty acres of land at Canford and another forty acres at Sturminster Marshall for three years, specifically to grow woad.

The cultivation of woad needed much labour, both in the preparation of the ground and tending the crop as well as in picking and processing the leaves - which had to be crushed in a mill and allowed to ferment before being rolled into balls and dried, after which it was ready to be sold to the dyers. When Bedford died in 1607, he left bequests to the poor of the parishes of Damerham, Martin, Pentridge and Cranborne 'in remembrance of my good will for theire labours and worke bestowed on my busyness'. Among other things, he also left 'Woade already grayned and in Balls, 18 Tonne' worth £400 and 'an olde woade house and fower woad mylles whereof two are at Martin and two at Blagdon' as well as five houses in Salisbury and a cloth mill at Laverstock. The importance of woad as a source of dye gradually declined with increasing imports of new dyes such as indigo and logwood.

Both the enlargement of sheep flocks and the development of new crops such as woad need to be seen in the context of the expansion of the woollen cloth industry in the west of England. Engagement in the industry offered the potential of large profits to be made by landlords, farmers and wool merchants.

In the fifteenth and sixteenth centuries, Sherborne was the centre of the Dorset woollen industry. Until then, the most important product of the industry was a woollen cloth made from short carded wool, felted by the fulling mill and finished by raising and shearing the nap to give a smooth surface in which warp and weft were completely united so that one would not be distinguished from the other. Some of the cloth was narrow but the characteristic cloth was broadcloth, from 54 to 63 inches wide. Before the 1630s, both Exeter and Lyme Regis relied on the export of what was known as the 'old draperies' in which the south-west specialised. In particular, they exported kersey cloth (often called 'dozens'), a cloth which was lighter than the traditional broadcloth and which had been evolved in the area in the sixteenth century.

From the 1630s, the export of the 'new draperies' as they were called became important. These were fabrics made from cheaper wool and although it was often spun into a fine yarn, the 'feel' of the material made from it was harsher than that of cloth made entirely from short, carding wool. One of the advantages of these new draperies and 'Spanish cloths' was that the fabric was of a lighter weight and had a particularly fine finish. Of these 'new draperies', the Dorset industry was producing, among other things, serges and bays. Cloth was produced for both home consumption and export (a large quantity was shipped to France), although there is little information as to what were the exact constituents of Dorset's woollen cloth export trade at this time.

By the eighteenth century, woollen cloth manufacture was conducted in the following centres: Beaminster, Bere Regis, Dorchester, Gillingham, Lyme Regis, Shaftesbury, Sturminster Newton and Wareham. No doubt it was the quality of the wool produced in Dorset which helped to ensure the survival of the Dorset industry. Wool Accounts at the Public Record Office for the mid-eighteenth century list a Dorset man from Marnhull offering 'choice

By the time this photograph was taken in 1914, Dorchester wool sales had become well-known due to the high quality of Dorset wool and attracted customers from all over the country.

locks' or 'superfine locks', which, by the end of the century, had become recognised names for the best sorts of wools. The decline of the woollen-cloth manufacturing industry in the period 1793-1815 was, in part at least, due to the impact of the war with France, and in particular to Napoleon's continental blockade which prevented exports to France, Germany and Holland, for example. With the resumption of peace, the cloth trade shifted to the steam-driven mills of Yorkshire.

Notwithstanding the decline of cloth manufacturing in Dorset - in 1812, woollen manufacture was confined to Sturminster Newton and Lyme Regis, the latter manufacturing broadcloth and flannel - the quality of the wool itself was, however, maintained well into the nineteenth century. This is illustrated by the well-known Dorset wool sales. According to advertisements appearing in the *Dorset County Chronicle* and *Somersetshire Gazette*, sales of wool by auction commenced in July 1881, when Mr T. Ensor held one in Dorchester and Blandford, followed by Henry Duke & Son in 1882. These sales

Flax mills tended to be built in the sheltered valleys of West Dorset, such as this one at Broadwindsor. The photograph was taken prior to the mill's demolition in 1970.

included the finest wools, mostly from Dorset Horn and Dorset Down breeds and soon became some of the most important of such sales in the country, attracting large numbers of buyers from what were by then the principal manufacturing centres in the north of England. In 1892, buyers came from Leicester and Halifax, among other places. The last recorded sales took place in 1939.

FLAX AND HEMP

The principal use for flax and hemp in Dorset was the manufacture of ropes, nets, twine and sailcoth for the fishing industry, a trade carried on for several hundred years over much of West Dorset and, in particular, at Bridport. In depth discussion of this aspect of the industry remains outside the scope of this book, but insofar as the growing of flax in Dorset was used for the manufacture of fabrics for clothing, it is an important topic in its own right.

There is documentary evidence for the growth and manufacture of

A retting tank at Slape Mills, near Netherbury in 1946. The retting process involves soaking the flax stalks in water in order to rot away the woody core, thus allowing the flax fibres to be loosened and removed.

hemp and flax in Bridport in the reign of King John in 1211, although the industry probably goes back well before this. The damp, mild and sheltered valleys of western Dorset with their light loam soils were ideal for the growing of hemp and flax and, at a time when the majority of clothing was made at home, much of the flax used for linen clothing (in particular undergarments) would have been spun and woven by women in the home on a domestic basis. With the coming of industrialisation, the streams of the area could be harnessed for water-power. These streams were also ideal for the 'retting' process: this involves soaking the flax stalks in water to rot away the woody core and to dissolve the gum so that the fibres can be loosened and pulled away.

After drying, the fibres are separated by 'swingling' before the flax or hemp is combed into parallel fibres by 'heckling'. By the late eighteenth century, the leading flax-producing parish in Dorset was Symondsbury, which by 1794 accounted for about a quarter of the total output of flax in Dorset. In 1803 Richard Roberts established

Female flax workers worked long shifts well into the twentieth century on low wages at mills such as Clenham Mill (about 1890).

Queed Mill, Netherbury, in 1915.

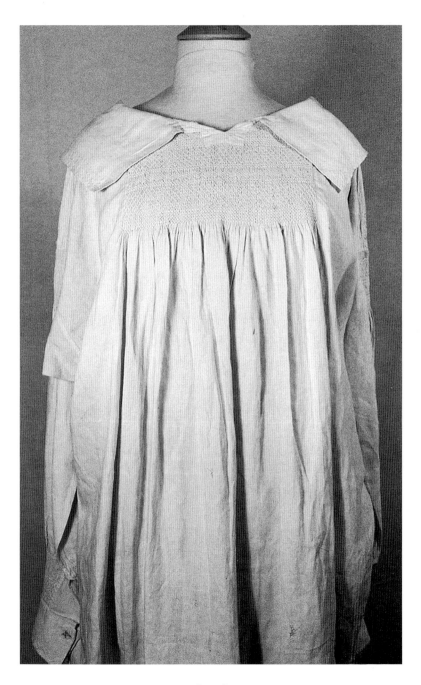

his swingling mill (also used for spinning) on a tributary of the River Bride in Burton Bradstock, south-east of the church. Set in a wall of what is now housing, is a stone inscribed: 'This flax-swingling mill, the first introduced into the West of England, was erected by Richard Roberts, 1803'. The erection of the mill partly explains the unemployment in the surrounding villages, as flax swingling by hand had previously been a great winter standby for labouring families.

Not far from the mill, Roberts erected a row of cottages for his weavers. At this time it was still possible for male workers to divide their time between work on smallholdings and at the loom, and the lives of those employed in the spinning mills were not entirely divorced from life on the land.

Wages for flax and hemp spinning were low: in her book *Bound to the Soil*, Barbara Kerr cites a Mrs Reed of Netherbury, who recounted how, as late as the 1880s, her mother tramped three miles to work a twelve-hour day in Pymore Mill, Bradpole, for 4s. a week. Mrs Reed herself followed in her mother's footsteps and worked at the turn of the twentieth century in Slape Mill, where, as an unskilled worker, she was paid 2s. 6d. a week, a sum which eventually rose to 7s. when she acquired more sophisticated spinning skills.

The flax and hemp industries remained important well into the nineteenth century. By then, even though a proportion of the raw material manufactured by Roberts and other manufacturers would still have been grown locally, much was by now being imported, in particular from Russia. Little is known about the products of Roberts' business although he described it as a 'general manufactory of sail cloth, duck, sheetings, table linen, napkins plain and figured, wrappings and packing cloths'.

The reference to 'duck' is noteworthy: although a term of disputed derivation, this was a fabric which was often used in relation to the making of smocks. In *Far from the Madding Crowd*, Thomas Hardy

Smock-frock of fine white linen or 'duck'. The smocking on the chest and wrists gave the garment a certain amount of elasticity, which made it comfortable and hard-wearing. Although difficult to date with any precision, this smock is likely to have been made no later than the middle decades of the nineteenth century. In general, fabric became coarser and embroidery more elaborate from the 1850s onwards.

refers to the labourers coming to receive their wages on Bathsheba Everdene's farm: 'They were, as usual, in snow-white smock-frocks of Russia duck, and some in whitey-brown ones of drabbet - marked on the wrists, breasts, backs and sleeves with honeycomb-work.'

Another fabric used for the making of smocks was dowlas (a coarse linen cloth), whose manufacture was continued at Cerne Abbas, Gillingham, Silton, and Bourton. At Bourton, linsey-wolsey (a rough cloth made of a linen warp and woollen weft) was also made. All but the coarsest linen was expensive, which accounts for the popularity of mixtures of fibres such as linsey-wolsey, which was used for, among other garments, aprons worn by working people. The expense of linen and the fact that it is relatively laborious to care for, as well as the expansion and industrialisation of the cotton industry, helps to explain the increasing popularity of cotton from the late eighteenth and early nineteenth centuries and the subsequent decline in the demand for linen.

THE SILK INDUSTRY

Although ribbons and some silks had been woven in London since the sixteenth century, the rapid growth of the English silk-weaving industry took place in the second half of the seventeenth century. By the eighteenth century it was centred in the Spitalfields area of London, where high quality plain and patterned silks were woven. Dynamism was given to the industry by the influx into the area of Huguenot refugees who fled their home countries during waves of persecution across the Channel. Furthermore, the incredible talent of English designers such as Anna Maria Garthwaite, Joseph Dandridge and James Leman contributed what must surely be some of the most beautiful patterns ever produced. (A number of these pattern books are now in the Victoria and Albert Museum in London).

In England, the silk industry was artificially protected from foreign competition until the 1820s. In 1699, the import, use and wearing of Indian and East Indian silks had been prohibited. Further fear of competition, this time from printed calicoes, led the Weavers' Company to mount a campaign for their prohibition. This was achieved in 1721. In 1826, however, restrictions prohibiting the

Eighteenth-century 'sack-back' gown of silk, originally given to the
Dorset County Museum by nieces of the Victorian philanthropist
and social reformer, the 7th Earl of Shaftesbury. The design is
typical of the delicate, floral designs popular at this time.

This remarkable late 1850s photograph shows the unidentified Dorset couple in unusually relaxed and informal poses for the period. The woman is fashionably dressed, with a tight-waisted and full-skirted watered-silk gown and the centre-parted hair is typical of the 1850s.

import of silks were lifted, and the consequence was a flood of French silks into the country. Many Spitalfields silk weavers went bankrupt and journeymen starved. At the same time, changes in fashion which led to the popularity of printed cottons meant that the English silk industry was doomed. Fashion was no longer to remain the preserve of the fashionable elite who could afford the most expensive silks, but was to come within the reach of the rapidly expanding middle classes and even the better-off sections of the working classes.

The changing fortunes of the English silk industry is, as would be expected, mirrored to a large extent in that of Dorset's silk industry, which dates from the mid-eighteenth century. The latter has always been chiefly concerned with the spinning ('throwing') of silk rather than with weaving and manufacture of the raw material. Silk throwing involves the threads of raw silk being twisted on the

Floral and striped silk ribbons, typical of the variety produced in the nineteenth century and used for trimming dresses and hats.

machines so that they become more substantial fibres. This was done on a 'mill', an improved form of which had been introduced at Derby in 1719 by Sir Thomas Lombe. After throwing, the silk was ready to be woven into either ribbon or broad silk.

Sherborne was to become the centre of the county's industry, although there was also silk-spinning at Gillingham and smaller concerns at Cerne Abbas and Stalbridge. According to Hutchins' *History of Dorset*, silk throwing commenced in 1740, when, it states, 'they erected mills on Sir Thomas Lombe's plan'. John Sharrer, a Spitalfields silk thrower, acquired the lease of a water grist-mill in Westbury, within the manor of Sherborne, sometime in the mid-eighteenth century, although the precise date is unknown. Sharrer had the original mill pulled down and replaced it with a building which dates from about 1755. Possible reasons for Sharrer's move to Sherborne include the following factors: he had relatives living in Sherborne; there was abundant water to supply the power for driving the machinery and, last but by no means least, there was sufficient labour to work the mills. Sharrer is said to have employed 500 hands in London; 200 in Gloucestershire; 400 in Cheshire and the same in Dorset. Of the total 1,500 employed by Sharrer, 1,400 were women and children.

Staff of Sherborne silk mill outside the factory in 1905. Four years earlier, the Census Returns of 1901 listed 116 women and 19 men employed in the industry, although it was certainly on the decline by this date.

Children were employed to undertake the simpler processes involved in the throwing of silk, such as the preliminary winding. Women and children employed in 1786 had previously been in receipt of parish relief. Therefore it comes as no surprise that the parish overseers, in the main, approved of the starting of a silk house since this meant a reduction in the poor rates. However, conditions for the workers themselves were unsatisfactory: for example, workers were generally paid for piece work and if trade was slack, this inevitably meant lower wages. In 1793, however, the weekly wages averaged at 1s. 5d. each for 48 winders. Although the majority of the industry was carried on at the mills, winders could carry on their trade at home and combine it with agricultural pursuits.

In 1764, Sharrer entered into a partnership agreement with his two nephews, George Ward of Sherborne and William Wilmott of Hornsey. Both nephews were silk throwers. On their uncle's death in

1769, Wilmott carried on silk throwing at Sherborne and at Cerne Abbas and Stalbridge, while Ward continued with the business already begun at Bruton in Somerset. In the main, the thrown silk was then taken to London for weaving. The Wilmott Records (kept in the Dorset County Record Office) reveal that Wilmott was supplying a Mr Sabatier, a master weaver based at Spitalfields: between February and May 1766 Sabatier sent to Wilmott a number of bales of silk of different sizes containing altogether 439 lbs 6ozs of raw Valentia silk which Wilmott threw at 2s. 6d. per pound (a total of £54 18s. 5d.). It appears that most of the silk prepared at Sherborne at this time was obtained from Italy and from China.

Prices, and therefore the profitability of silk throwing, were seriously affected by the introduction of foreign thrown silk as well as the severe competition posed by the influx of French manufactures in the 1820s. Nevertheless, the Dorset silk industry seems to have survived remarkably well and was continued by William Wilmott's descendants. According to the 1901 Census Returns, 116 women and 19 men were still employed at this date in the silk industry. A few years later, the *Victoria County History* reported that:

'silk throwing is still a principal feature of the craft, but silk weaving is now undertaken at Sherborne where many new looms have been set up by Messrs. J. and R. Wilmott. Further improvements are contemplated, but the industry is handicapped by the sudden changes of fashion and by the variations in the yield of silk crops, these difficulties naturally pressing more heavily on a small than on a large industry.'

TEXTILE AND CLOTHING
CRAFTS AND TRADES

GLOVEMAKING

Little is known about those textile trades and industries which provided essential accessories for the wealthier classes or, just as important, an element of luxury in a life otherwise lacking in all but the most basic clothing. This ignorance is accounted for by the fact that few records survive relating to these industries, not least because they were mostly conducted by women working at home.

Most is known about the gloving industry, although the fame of the Dorset trade is eclipsed by that of its neighbour across the county border in Somerset. In 1908, when the Yeovil industry was at its height, no topographer includes gloving among the local industries of the county. As the Dorset *Victoria County History* points out:

> Some clue to the apparent oversight may be gathered from the fact that the more important glove-making centre of Yeovil was within easy reach, and it is probable that, even at a very early date, the Dorset glovers were chiefly employees of those of Somerset, rather than manufacturers on their own account.

Some of the earliest references to glove-making in Dorset are in documents relating to Bridport in connection with glovers overcharging during the fifteenth and sixteenth centuries. Gloves were then either of leather decorated with lavish embroidery, spangles and ribbons (given as costly presents), or they were simpler leather gloves used for everyday wear. Trends in gloves tended to complement the history of fashion. For example, in the eighteenth century, with the fashion for elbow-length sleeves, gloves became longer. When women adopted the high-waisted, short-sleeved fashions of the 1790s, gloves extended well above the elbow and were often secured by drawstrings or ribbon ties. By the mid-nineteenth century, gloves were closer fitting due to improvements in sizing as well as to the introduction of buttons and snap fasteners to secure them.

During the nineteenth century, centres of gloving included Beaminster, Cerne Abbas and Bere Regis. The industry was conducted largely on a domestic basis: in a number of cases, the leather glove pieces were sent over from Yeovil and Milborne Port to be sewn by women in their own homes. For women, this arrangement had the advantage of enabling them to look after children at the same time as earning money and to supplement their earnings from glove-making by working on the land, especially during the harvest and at haymaking. Thomas Hardy's mother, Jemima Hardy, was one of many women who did gloving (glove embroidery in her case), to earn a little extra money.

From as early as the fifteenth century, the glove trade had been protected by legislation preventing the importation of foreign-made gloves. In particular, the trade received a boost in 1766 when it was decreed that 'any foreign manufactured leather gloves or mitts might be searched for by any customs or excise officer and, when found, seized'. Furthermore, those found in possession of imported gloves were liable to a fine of £200. The lifting of restrictions in 1826, (which allowed the influx of foreign-made gloves), caused widespread unemployment and suffering for those whose livelihood was dependent on gloving. This is reflected in the fact that a number of those receiving poor relief in, for example, the Yeovil workhouses in the 1830s were recorded as being glovers.

Nevertheless, the industry managed to survive, not least because of the important part gloves played in the Victorian obsession with the conventions of fashion and, more especially, with the notion of 'etiquette'. For middle class women, the warmth provided by gloves was probably of less importance than the fact that they protected delicate white hands from the bronzing rays of the sun. Furthermore, well-chosen gloves which coordinated with an outfit enhanced a fashionable and 'respectable' appearance.

For men, too, gloves formed an important element of a well-groomed appearance. In his book, *The Whistler at the Plough*, the writer, Alexander Somerville, describes passing through the Wiltshire town of Westbury in the 1840s and seeing a man outside the bank:

'There is the bank right opposite the inn; and there is, standing right in front of the bank, a young gentleman with moustachios and an imperial, a white beaver, kid gloves, and a superfine royal cigar, scented and scenting the morning air; that he belongs to the bank is as sure as the ornamental painting of the door.'

A number of different kinds of gloves were probably made in Dorset: lamb, kid and goat gloves for fashionable and close-fitting garments. In addition, there is evidence of coarser, funtional gloves being made, including heavier, shapeless thumbed gloves worn primarily for warmth and protection by hedgers while working. Furthermore, in the Dorset villages on the Hampshire border, Ringwood gloves, knitted of soft string, were made by cottagers. More traditional knitted gloves were also made on a domestic basis, often by young girls who would learn to knit from an early age. The rates of pay in the 1880s were 6½d. for a pair knitted with 'Berlin' wool, 5d. for ordinary wool and 5½d. for cotton.

Although statistics for Dorset are hard to come by, those for Somerset give us some idea of the scale of the industry at this time. By the mid 1850s records show that an average of 4,600 dozen pairs of gloves were being made weekly in Yeovil, with a further 3,500 pairs in the neighbourhood, including the Dorset villages just over the county border, providing employment for more than 10,000 men, women and children. Wages varied enormously, with men - who generally did the cutting and the dressing of the leather - paid the most (from 21s. to 30s. a week). Women and children did the sewing and were paid by the dozen pairs of gloves (4s. to 6s. per week for women and 1s. to 2s. 6d. per week for children).

Employers were exacting and women worked very long hours. There were penalties for poor or 'dirty' work. Before the advent of the sewing machine in the mid-nineteenth century, most gloving cottages would have had a device known as the 'donkey frame', which had been patented by James Winter of Stoke-Sub-Hamdon (Somerset) in 1807. This was a small, vice-like arrangement with fine teeth, mounted on a stand. The worker opened or closed the teeth by means of a treadle, fixing the glove so that the edges were held firmly together. She then passed her needle in and out of the teeth and a

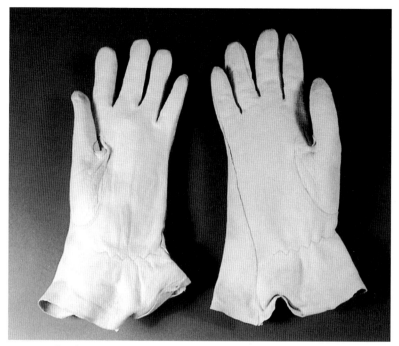

Stalbridge gloves made in the twentieth century. In the 1860s, a
commission into women and children's employment reported that at
Stalbridge, 'girls go early to gloving, which is misery to them as long as
they live. They are put down to it as soon as they can hold a needle'.

perfectly regular stitch resulted. The frame or 'engine' as it was
sometimes called, enabled workers to produce work of a consistent
standard. The number of stitches per inch was usually 18-20,
although it could sometimes be as many as 32.

With the adoption of the sewing-machine from the mid-nineteenth
century, women outworkers could either try to loan a machine from
their employer (who would make a deduction for depreciation or pay
a lower piece rate), but in so doing they were then restricted in
working only for him. Alternatively, women could try to save up to
buy their own machines. In either case, working in badly ventilated
cottages in cramped conditions and poor lighting was one of the
hazards of outworking. The parliamentary commissioner for Dorset
reporting on the 'employment of children, young persons and women

in agriculture' in 1867 blamed gloving for the neglect of young girls' education and, later, for older girls not going into domestic service:

'Throughout the (Blackmore) Vale, and in some other parts of the county, as in the neighbourhood of Blandford, the manufacture of gloves is carried on to a considerable extent, by the families of the agricultural labourers. It is very unremunerative work, and can only be made to pay by long hours of very hard work, and, like most other domestic duties of this description, it involves the younger members of the family being kept at home from a very early age, being put to work as soon as they can hold a needle, and being afterwards kept away from service.'

By the early twentieth century, 45 men and 631 women were recorded working at the trade in Dorset. 'Glove-sewing', according to the *Victoria County History*, 'ranks next to the hemp industry in providing work for Dorset women, but it is not nearly so widespread, nor so independent, as it would not be hard at any moment for the manufacturers to have their gloves sewn elsewhere'. In Bere Regis, gloving had taken the place of buttony from the mid-nineteenth century, continuing there until the First World War. Meanwhile, the centres of the Dorset gloving industry had become Sherborne and Gillingham. The organisation of the industry had undergone changes too. In Sherborne, three factories carried glove-making through all its stages, from the preparation and dressing of skins, to the cutting out of the gloves and their sewing, stitching, buttoning and finishing.

Gloving came to Sherborne in 1871 when Adam Stewart and William Blake went into partnership and started a business in Cheap Street. In 1880 the partnership ended and each went into business on their own. Around the turn of the century, James Seager, an employee of Adam Stewart started up another gloving business. A few inhabitants of Sherborne still remember beginning work in their teens in the glove factory in Sherborne in the 1930s, where they worked from 8am until 6pm, girls receiving 7s. 6d. a week in wages.

Over the course of the twentieth century, fashions underwent huge changes and with the growing informality of clothing, gloves gradually lost much of their former appeal as essential fashion accessories and became functional necessities. The decline of the industry reflected these changes.

Handmade lace is of two types: bobbin lace made on a hard cushion or pillow (hence its other name, 'pillowlace'), with threads weighted by wood or bone bobbins, or needle lace made with a needle and thread using a variety of buttonhole stitches. Both types were probably introduced into England through trade links with Flanders (Belgium) during the second half of the sixteenth century.

Like gloves, lace was a fashion accessory for many hundreds of years. It was made into the most exquisite collars, cuffs, sleeves and trimmings, for example. Lacemaking was labour-intensive: this meant the finished item was extremely expensive and it could therefore be afforded only by the wealthier members of society and worn as a status-symbol. The increased demand for lace as a fashionable commodity is reflected in the cost: in 1594, bone lace could be bought at 1s. 4d. per yard whereas in 1685 the prices had increased, ranging from 2s. 4d. to 30s.

Bobbin lacemaking became a widespread cottage industry, particularly in the West Country, and in Bedfordshire, Buckingham-shire and Northamptonshire. The industry in Dorset is much less

Before the advent of machine-made lace, many women of all classes made lace at home, many of them using lace patterns such as these.

Lace-makers outside their cottages in Sherborne Lane, Lyme Regis, in the 1880s.

well-known than that of Devon, although when Daniel Defoe visited the county in 1705, he wrote that Blandford was 'chiefly famous for making the finest bone-lace in England': 'they showed me some so exquisitely fine as I think I never saw better in Flanders, France or Italy, and which they said they rated at above £30 sterling a yard'.

In the eighteenth and early nineteenth centuries, pillow lacemaking was carried out in a number of towns and villages, including Sherborne, Lyme Regis, and Charmouth. Broad Street in Lyme Regis in 1750 was chiefly inhabited by lacemakers. A familiar sight would have been women sitting in their doors in the summer working at their lace. Presumably, working outside was preferable to being confined in damp and badly-ventilated cottages. The parliamentary commissioner reporting on women and children's employment in 1843 wrote of its ill-effects, comparing it unfavourably to field-work:

'I have seen the effects of lace-making, straw-plaiting, and button-making, and I have no hesitation in saying that there are many diseases proceeding from the confinement of young persons in crowded rooms, the keeping of the body constantly in an unnatural position, and the incessant call upon the utmost power of the eye, which these trades require. Thousands of children of agricultural labourers are employed at these species of work. However much I am opposed to field-labour, there is infinitely less physical injury to be feared from it than from employments of the nature spoken of above.'

Like other craft-based industries, the advent of machine-made lace from the mid-nineteenth century was to be one of the contributory factors in the subsequent decline of lace as a fashion item and therefore as an employer of female and child labour.

HABERDASHERY AND HOSIERY

With the widespread availability of ready-made, 'off-the-peg' clothing today, it is easy to forget the former importance of haberdashery (clothing accessories and dressmaking aids) when the majority of clothing was made by the village dressmaker or at home. During the course of the eighteenth century, as its cloth trade gradually declined, Sherborne became an important centre for the production of haberdashery. Not only did the town supply a local clientele, but also markets further afield throughout the west of England.

In addition, there were small pockets of industry, such as that of ribbon-weaving in Cranborne in the eighteenth century. While Bridport was known principally for its ropes, nets and twine, linen thread was also made there (used for the sewing of smocks, for example). Melbury Osmond was noted in the early part of the nineteenth century for the manufacture of staymakers' tape, known as 'Melbury iron tape'. Although there are few records relating to these industries, they must have provided at least a certain amount of regular employment, not to mention much-needed goods.

Hosiery, another staple of both men and women's wardrobes of all classes, was an important industry in Dorset. The term hosiery comes from the word 'hose' (close-fitting coverings for the legs worn from the Middle Ages until the seventeenth century) and was used to refer to both men's and women's garments. Those worn by women were secured by garters at or above the knees whereas men's hose were longer, being attached to the waistband of the drawers. The more widely-known term 'stocking' came into use in the sixteenth century. Men continued to wear stockings with breeches well into the nineteenth century, although the fashion for trousers eventually ousted them from men's wardrobes, whereas for women, stockings only began to lose their popularity with the availability of more convenient tights in the 1960s.

Hand-knitted stockings were much worn until the late eighteenth century. However, after William Lee's invention of the stocking frame in 1589, fine stockings could easily be produced by machine, installed in small workshops or in knitters' own homes, until the coming of increased mechanisation and factory production in the 1870s and 1880s. In Dorset, as with other crafts, stocking knitting took place largely on a domestic basis. Until the twentieth century, the range was limited to either wool, cotton, linen or silk stockings.

In Dorset, silk stockings were being made at Poole in the 1750s and cotton yarn was spun at Abbotsbury in 1750 for the manufacture of stockings. Wimborne and the surrounding area was well-known for the quality of its stockings. In Wimborne itself in 1793, a large number of women and children were engaged in knitting worsted stockings, the worsted costing from 2d. to 2½d. per oz., the finished stocking selling at from 3s. 6d. to 4s. per pair.

According to Daniel Defoe, Stalbridge stockings were 'the finest, best and highest prized in England'. As with other craft-based industries, the introduction of sophisticated machinery into the industry dealt the final blow to this as well as to other home industries.

BUTTONY

Referring to Blandford in 1823, Pigot's *Trade Directory* stated that the 'principal support of the town and neighbouring villages, is the manufacture of thread, waistcoat and shirt buttons, which employs several hundred women and children'. In Shaftesbury, the picture was the same: 'the principal manufacture is the making of all kinds of shirt buttons; those of inferior quality are made at the low price of five pence per gross of 12 dozen, the labourer finding thread'. The 1843 Parliamentary Commission of Enquiry into the 'Employment of Women and Children in Agriculture' referred to the importance of button-making as a local industry, claiming that it was followed by 'nearly all the labourers' wives and children above 6 years old' and that 'the earnings of a family at button-making amount to 3s., 4s., 5s. and sometimes 6s., or even more a week'.

Fewer than twenty years later, however, the story is very different. As Pigot's states, 'the manufacture of shirt buttons, which formerly was carried on extensively in the town and its vicinity, has, of late years, very much declined'. By 1865, J. G. Harrod's *Postal and Commercial Directory* ceased listing any shirt button wire manufacturers at all. One of the principal reasons for the rapid decline of the industry was the introduction of machinery which threatened directly the profitability of the hand-made product.

The question is frequently asked, why did the making of these buttons originally take place in Dorset? One of the possible explanations is that Dorset and, in particular, the Shaftesbury area – around and in which the industry became concentrated – provided good quantities of horn, from the Dorset Horn sheep. The horn was

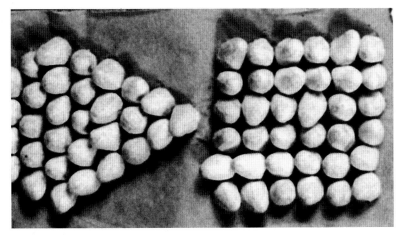
Dorset buttons of the 'high top' variety.

used for the flat circular base of the buttons before the introduction of wire rings. Furthermore, as with other industries, fluctuations in employment meant that the wives and children of farm labourers needed and were available for alternative employment.

As with so many innovations, the explanation for the success of the Dorset button industry lies in the unique circumstances surrounding its development. It is generally accepted that the founder of the Dorset button industry was Abraham Case, who came from a family of Cotswold yeomen farmers. Having served as a soldier on the Continent – where he probably saw the work of French and Belgian button-makers – Case settled in 1622 with his new wife in a cottage in Shaftesbury, where he began to explore the possibility of setting up a button manufactory. The fashion at this time for well-fitting, expensive and elaborately embroidered waistcoats for men and lavishly decorated dresses for women undoubtedly encouraged the use of the button both as a functional fastening device, as well as a form of decoration.

Initially, Abraham Case restricted his production to the 'high top', a button made from a disc of sheep's horn with a hole in the centre, covered in linen on which a delicate wax-threadwork pattern was worked to make a conical button. An example of Case's own work can apparently be seen on the silk waistcoat worn by Charles I at his execution and preserved at Longleat House. It is likely that these buttons were also used on women's dresses.

The rare black 'singleton' buttons were the only coloured buttons produced by the firm at any stage in its history: it seems they were only made between 1658 and 1682. The story goes that Abraham's widow, inconsolable at the death of her husband, continued to make only black buttons up to the time of her own death. The firm – which had, in 1660, established its first 'branch' outside Shaftesbury (in Bere Regis) - was taken over by Abraham's sons and grandsons, but there were continual quarrels between the sons, Abraham and Elias. Added to this were problems related to competition for labour. By the early eighteenth century, there were 700 women and children working at buttony, either in their own cottages or at one of the firm's establishments. Local farmers needed workers too and there could be severe friction at busy times of the farming calendar, in particular at harvest time.

Both these problems, as well as the growing demand for high quality buttons at home and abroad, necessitated reorganisation of the business. In 1731, the firm engaged John Clayton, an astute businessman from York. Clayton recommended that button production should be entrusted almost exclusively to outworkers who would spend their time on button-making or on harvesting as they chose, but they would only be paid for buttons made to the firm's standard of quality. Furthermore, Clayton realised that all sales, marketing and financial business would be better dealt with from a London office rather than from isolated Dorset villages. Accordingly, an office was opened at 19 Addle Street, London, in 1743. To deal with foreign orders and export, the firm also opened a small office in Liverpool. Case's Street and Clayton Square in Liverpool were built by Peter Case (Abraham Case's grandson) on the profits of the button trade.

Meanwhile, in Dorset, depots were established in a number of villages including Wool, Sixpenny Handley, Piddletrenthide, Langton Matravers and Lytchett Minster (the latter was on the site of what is now the Old Button Shop Antiques). The central depot was established in 1803 at Milborne Stileham, a hamlet of Milborne St. Andrew. All depots were attended by agents on a particular day each

Button workers outside the old button depot, Lytchett Minster, 1900.

week when outworkers would bring in their products and collect fresh supplies of raw materials. (Interestingly, until 1800, the firm paid their workers in goods rather than in cash.) 'Button Day' in those villages where depots had been established must have been an exciting event. On a predetermined day each week, the agent would arrive with raw materials and payment in return for the finished buttons brought in by outworkers, who may well have walked more than ten miles to deliver the finished buttons.

Children were employed at the depots at Shaftesbury and Bere Regis to prepare the raw materials ready for collection by the outworkers. The wires or rings were made from rust-resistant wire (which came from Birmingham). The wire was burned, and twisted on a spindle, the nipped ends put together and soldered by expert girls or boys called 'Winders and Dippers'. 'Stringers' counted the rings and threaded them in lots of 144. These rings were used for the wheel-type buttons (the 'cross-wheel', 'Blandford cartwheel' and 'honeycomb'). The women at the depots were employed to clean the finished buttons: soiled buttons would be placed in a linen bag and boiled clean. They were then sorted and mounted on coloured card according to the quality of the work. Yellow card was used for what

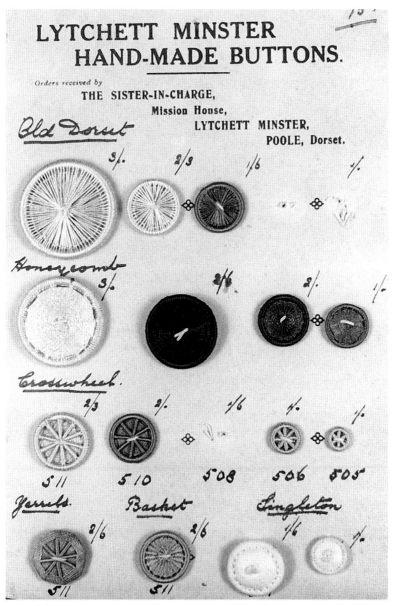

LYTCHETT MINSTER HAND-MADE BUTTONS.

Orders received by

THE SISTER-IN-CHARGE,
Mission House,
LYTCHETT MINSTER,
POOLE, Dorset.

Old Dorset

3/.   2/9   1/6   1/.

Honeycomb

3/.   2/6   2/.   1/.

Crosswheel.

2/3   2/.   1/6   1/.   1/.

511   510   508   506   505

Jarrots.   *Basket*   *Singleton*

2/6   2/6   1/6   1/.

511   511

A card of various Dorset buttons made by traditional techniques by the Lytchett Mission in the twentieth century. Buttons such as these were hand-worked on rust-resistant rings.

'Dorset knobs' were flatter than the traditional 'high tops' and gave their name to the Dorset biscuit of the same name.

would today be called 'seconds'. Blue card was used for standard quality buttons and pink card for best quality. Only the buttons on pink or blue cards were exported. The 'seconds' were sold locally at reduced prices.

While some people were employed at the depots, the majority of workers were employed as outworkers. Women worked in their cottages, making buttons at between 1s. 6d. and 4s. per gross (much less for seconds). There is also evidence of buttony being undertaken by workhouse inmates, which was, no doubt, considered to be 'respectable' employment. For example, in Blandford workhouse by 1770 there were three men and eleven women engaged wholly in button-making for the Case firm, with an average of ten gross of buttons being produced each day. In addition, some charity schools taught children the art of buttony. Towards the end of the eighteenth century, Lady Caroline Damer established a school at Milton Abbas for 12 poor children, who were clothed and taught reading, and instructed first in spinning, and afterwards in making buttons.

By the early nineteenth century there was said to be a wide range of over one hundred different types of button in production, of which the best known is the 'Dorset knob'. These were similar to the 'high tops', but were flatter. Although the firm achieved its highest turnover in 1807 (£14,000), the death of Clayton and the subsequent inheritance of the business by two brothers in 1803 brought about

After the decline of the Case business, Dorset buttons continued to be made by the Lytchett Mission until 1915. In this photograph, button workers stand outside South Lytchett Manor, in about 1900.

some disruption to the business. Even so, at this time, button-making as a cottage industry embraced the greater part of East Dorset with 4000 people employed. The subsequent collapse of the industry was to cause severe hardship to many families.

Although industrialisation had brought with it the development of the metal button industry, centred, in particular, in the Midlands, the impact of potential competition was not felt until the mid-nineteenth century. At the Great Exhibition at Crystal Palace in 1851, a machine for making buttons was displayed, which eventually dealt the death-blow to the hand-made button industry in Dorset. The story was told by Samuel Case:

'Perhaps you would like to learn something of Ashton's Patent Machine for making buttons and the disastrous effect on the locally made button. It was the year of the Great Exhibition that it was whispered among the people of

East Dorset (for there were only a few stray buttoners west of Puddletown) and the smash came at last. 1851-2-3 worse and worse; we employed in wire makers, paperers and button makers from 800-1000 but they were soon in a state of poverty, some starving, and hundreds were sent off to Perth, Moreton Bay and Quebec by the noblemen of the county, about 350 left Shaftesbury.... My uncle and father dissolved partnership and in 1849-50 there was on hand a stock of £14,500 worth of goods and buttons, but my uncle still continued his journeys to the chief towns. Ashton's buttons were becoming known everywhere, but I may state that in March 1859 I sold in the city £856 worth of wire and cloth-worked buttons in five days, all to be delivered within a month of purchase; and that was the last extensive sale of the hand-worked button. My father was just on being ruined, but the lords of the manors of Bere Regis and Milborne stepped into the breach and saved him.'

The family business finally ended with the death of Henry Case. Some buttons continued to be made and were sold from what is now the Old Button Shop Antiques in Lytchett Minster, the work undertaken by the Lytchett Mission until 1915.

CLOTHES AND THE RURAL POOR

FASHIONABLE AND FUNCTIONAL CLOTHING

So far, this book has largely considered clothing and textile goods made by the poor for the wealthy. Although I have described the numerous skills needed to make fabrics and clothing accessories, and the important income they provided both to employers and workers, it would be leaving out a crucial part of the story of Dorset's textiles not to write about the clothing worn by those who spent much of their time making clothing for others.

Researching this subject is problematic. The clothing belonging to the poorer majority of the population in Dorset - as in most other rural counties - was subjected to constant wear and tear and, as a consequence, does not survive in great quantities. In his novel *Tess of*

Ploughing at Swanage in about 1910. The man wears a simple, smock-like garment and the subdued hue of his clothing reflects the fact that the clothes of the poor were subject to constant wear and tear, as well as exposure to the elements when working out-of-doors.

William Churchill, a Crimean War veteran, wears an unusual indigo -dyed smock. The stitching forming the smocking is coming undone: clothing was worn until it wore out. Many poor people had only one set of working clothes, and if they were fortunate, a set of clothes for special occasions and Sunday best.

the d'Urbervilles (1891), Thomas Hardy describes how Tess's clothing – 'a gray serge cape, a red woollen cravat, a stuff skirt covered by a whitey-brown rough wrapper, and buff leather gloves' – has been constantly subjected to the elements: 'every thread of that old attire has become faded and thin under the stroke of raindrops, the burn of sunbeams, the stress of winds'.

People very often did not have a change of clothing and going to bed in damp clothes must have been a common occurrence. Thomas

Beige silk bodice and skirt, probably worn as a wedding/going-away outfit
in the 1880s. The wealthier classes living in Dorset had a considerable
amount of contact with centres of fashion such as London and Paris and
the styles of their clothes reflected the silhouette of high fashion: in the
1880s, this was a tightly-fitting bodice (worn over a tightly-laced corset)
and skirt with the fullness centred at the back and worn over a bustle.

Hardy's own father visited Bath in 1877 in the hope of curing the rheumatism contracted as a result of never bothering to take off wet clothes when he came home from work. Furthermore, the clothes of the poor were sometimes deliberately destroyed in order to halt the spread of infection. For example, during the cholera outbreak of 1854, Henry Moule, Vicar of Fordington (at that time an extremely poor part of Dorchester), organised the boiling or burning of clothes and linen of those who had died, in order to halt the further spread of infection. In these circumstances, it is no wonder that few such clothes survive.

The middle and upper classes, on the other hand, had a much larger wardrobe, did not do the same dirty jobs and tended to hold onto their clothes because they were made of expensive fabric, or were richly embroidered, making them valuable and more likely to be cared for properly. In spite of the unlikelihood of their survival, examples of clothing belonging to working people can, amazingly, be found.

The Dorset County Museum has a wealth of surviving examples of dress. These include fashionable items of clothing which have connections to members of the local Dorset gentry, such as a mid-eighteenth century open robe and petticoat (skirt) of silk brocade, given to the Museum by the nieces of the philanthropist and social reformer, the 7th Earl of Shaftesbury (see page 23). The 'sack-back' style of the bodice and fullness of the skirt is typical of its time and garments such as these reflect the fact that fashion - for those who could afford it - was just as accessible whether you lived in Dorset or any other rural county.

By the late eighteenth century, the availability of fashion plates and magazines and the fact that members of the gentry would have been likely to spend part or all of the 'season' in London, meant that ideas and information about the latest fashions were never going to be far away. But for rich and poor alike, clothes were generally made by a dressmaker, tailor, or at home. Ready-made clothing was not widely available until the latter half of the nineteenth century.

Clothes worn by the well-off generally followed the style of high fashion, but for the vast majority, fashion was rarely the primary consideration. Although some items of clothing worn by working

A thatcher at work, Burton Bradstock, 1935. Just visible are his knee-pads and thatcher's 'palm' for protecting the hand when pushing in spars.

people followed the general style of fashionable clothing, they were, first and foremost, functional and worn for protection, depending on the particular occupation of the wearer. For example, thatchers wore a 'thatcher's palm' and knee-pads, the former to protect the hand when pushing in the spars to secure the thatch, the latter to protect the knees when kneeling against the thatch. In the novel *The Return of the Native* (1878), Thomas Hardy describes Clym Yeobright as a furze-cutter on Egdon Heath in the 'regulation dress of the craft': leggings, thick boots and leather gloves.

From the late eighteenth century until at least the 1880s, many Dorset working men - from carters to shepherds - wore a smock-frock over their clothes. Indeed, smocks were worn in rural areas throughout the southern counties and in the Midlands. When the smock-frock first appeared, it was worn over a linen or cotton shirt, breeches (made either of leather or corduroy) and leggings or gaiters and hard-wearing hob-nailed boots. William Cobbett, in his famous account of his travels around England, *Rural Rides* (1830), recalls wearing a smock as a child:

'I, with two brothers, used occasionally to desport ourselves, as the lawyers call it, at this sand-hill. Our diversion was this: we used to go to the top of the hill, which was steeper than the roof of a house; one used to draw his arms out of the sleeves of his smock-frock, and lay himself down with his arms by his sides; and then the others, one at head and the other at feet, sent him rolling down the hill like a barrel or a log of wood.'

From the 1820s, trousers (instead of breeches) were more common and were worn with leggings to protect the trousers. Shaftesbury Museum has a pair of leather straps, or 'yarks' which in the absence of leggings held up the trousers by fastening above the knees and so kept wet trousers away from the lower leg. Alternatively, if neither leggings or 'yarks' could be afforded, a piece of string could be ingeniously strapped round the leg below the knee in order to keep the hems of the trousers from getting muddy.

The smock-frock was essentially an outer garment, worn not only to protect (and perhaps conceal) the ragged clothing underneath, but, it was also, in its heyday, the quintessential garment of rural fashion. Made from white or natural linen ('duck') or a coarser twilled cotton and linen fabric called 'drabbet', smock-frocks kept out the wind and rain, and there is evidence that some attempts at waterproofing smocks were made by using linseed oil. Smock-frocks were also comfortable, the smocking on the chest, shoulder and cuff areas so typical of the garment giving the fabric a degree of 'elasticity'.

When smock-frocks were first worn, they were fairly simple garments, made from rectangular pieces of fabric, the shape being made by the smocking or 'honeycomb work' as Hardy so appositely referred to it. The design and execution of smocks display the needlework and creative skills of their makers. The *Dorset County*

Working clothing was functional as this photograph illustrates: the unidentified man wears a worn cardigan, waistcoat, corduroy trousers and billycock hat. He has tied the legs of the trousers under the knees to keep them from dragging in the mud. Note the well-worn boots with no laces.

Chronicle (14 September 1854) announced the prizes for a competition for 'handiwork at schools and shows': 'The woman who shall produce the best smock-frock, her own work, 7s., to Mary Ann Ayles, Bradford'. At this time, the majority of smocks were made at home by wives and children, although Hardy hints at the increasing availability of the ready-made item, when he describes Gabriel Oak, at the hiring-fair at Casterbridge (Dorchester) going to 'a ready-made clothes shop, the owner of which had a large rural connection,' and exchanging his overcoat for 'a shepherd's regulation smock-frock'.

By the mid-nineteenth century, many smocks were elaborately embroidered and a number of such smocks survive at the Dorset County Museum. They reflect the accuracy of Hardy's description in *Under the Greenwood Tree* (1872) of 'snow-white smock-frocks, embroidered upon the shoulders and breasts in ornamental forms of hearts, diamonds and zig-zags'.

Although it used to be thought that the particular design of the embroidery reflected the occupation of the wearer, there is little concrete evidence to back up this theory. Nevertheless, a high proportion of smocks with designs of hearts on them were said to have been worn at weddings. While these examples reveal a romantic association between the design of a smock and the occasion on which it was worn, the majority of motifs were probably chosen for their aesthetic merit or for the fact that they followed a traditional design in that particular family. Some are very beautiful.

The Dorset County Museum has over a dozen smocks, the majority of which are the typical 'round smock' variety (that is, they are the same front and back). While some survive in good condition, others are torn and stained, not surprising given their age and the number of times they must have been worn. The numerous mends and darns as well as the hand-stitched, selvedge seams serve as a reminder to us in our time of 'throwaway fashions,' of the value and importance of fabric (nothing was wasted), and of making clothes last. A number of the smocks have large, voluminous pockets, which would have carried a variety of important, everyday items. For example, Gabriel Oak's smock-frock pockets in *Far From the Madding Crowd* are deep enough to carry his flute.

Although little is known about the majority of smocks which

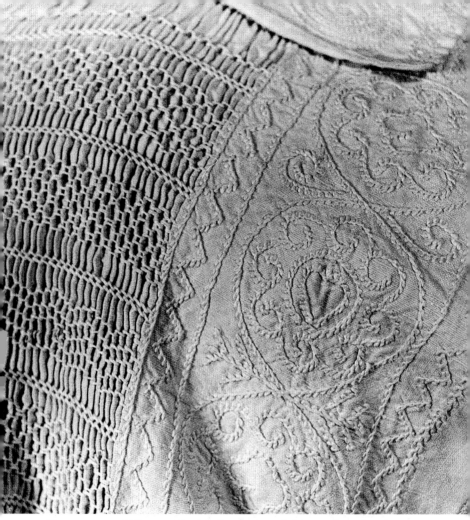

The accuracy of Thomas Hardy's description of the smocking detail on a smock-frock as 'honeycomb work' can clearly be seen on this smock. The heart design was a typical motif for the embroidery and links the making of the smock with the occasion for which it was to be worn, in this case, a wedding.

survive, the Dorset County Museum is fortunate to have more information than is usual about several of its smocks. For example, the owner and wearer of two of the smocks in the collection was Amalek Old of Wooton Glanville. Born in 1827, Amalek was apprenticed in 1844 at the age of 17 to Henry Guppy, blacksmith.

Amalek Old was born in 1827 at Wootton Glanville.
Two of the smocks belonging to him survive at the
Dorset County Museum.

The indenture still survives and states that Amalek should be provided with 'good, sufficient and proper diet and lodging, together with a proper apron yearly'.

An unusual short smock kept by the Dorset County Museum was owned and worn by Job Green, a West Dorset shepherd, who was born in 1814 in Toller Porcorum. The smock was made by his wife and is hand-sewn throughout. The absence of smocking on shoulders and chest is unusual (although there is smocking at the cuffs) as is the design of the embroidery, which depicts the Prince of Wales Feathers on the front and the words 'Ich Dien' ('I serve'). The Duchy of Cornwall, which continues to provide the Prince of Wales with an income, has substantial estates in Dorset, which may explain the choice of design. It is rare to find both the garment, and a photograph of it being worn by the owner, so these are particularly treasured.

Smocks had a multitude of purposes and could be worn on a number of different occasions. While the smocks described so far were generally worn for work, a number of the finer, whiter and intricately embroidered smocks would have been worn for special

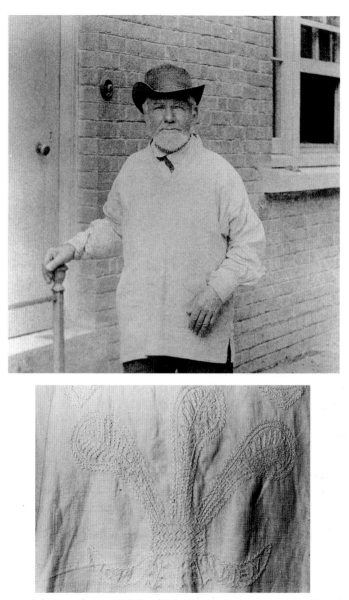

The top photograph is of Job Green wearing an unusual
short 'smock' embroidered with the Prince of Wales
feathers and the words 'Ich dien' ('I serve'), seen in the
detail in the lower photograph.

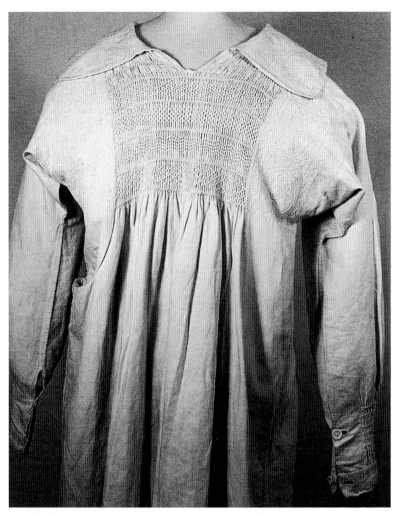

'Round' smock-frock of linen or 'duck', mid-late nineteenth century.

occasions, namely for weddings and for Sunday best. They would also have been worn for dressing up: a smock at the Dorset County Museum was worn by Dorset mummers during their performances: it was last used at Chetnole around 1910 by a Mr H. J. Penny. During the serialization of *The Return of the Native*, Thomas Hardy corresponded in 1878 with his illustrator, Arthur Hopkins, about the

Child's smock of linen, late nineteenth century.

kind of dress appropriate for the illustration of the mummers' scene:

'I think you have chosen well for the May illustration - certainly the incident after the mumming, with the mummers looking on, will be better than the mumming performance itself. Eustacia in boy's clothes, though pleasant enough to the imagination, would perhaps be unsafe as a picture. The sketch of a mummer's dress which I sent was merely intended to show the general system on which they used to decorate themselves: the surcoat or tunic was formed of a white smock-frock rather shorter than usual, tied in round the waist by a strap - this was almost invariably the groundwork of the costume. . .'

A number of older men and children went on wearing smock-frocks into the 1890s and even into the twentieth century. For example, a child's natural linen smock in the Dorset County Museum was made for the donor's grandfather when he was about three years

High West Street, Dorchester in the 1880s. This photograph was taken around the same time as Thomas Hardy wrote of the changes in traditional styles of dress in his essay, 'The Dorsetshire Labourer' (1883). In spite of Hardy's observations about the growing uniformity of rural dress, and the absence of any smocks, this photograph is interesting for its variety of clothing, depending on age, gender and class – ranging from the children in their pinafores on the left of the picture; the woman in the sun-bonnet in the centre; the well-dressed man in a suit with his back to us (to her right); to the older, poorer men on the far right in trousers, waistcoats and jackets.

old in 1895. In his essay, 'The Dorsetshire Labourer' (1883), Hardy noted that the smock-frock was becoming less popular for younger men. Comparing the scene at the annual hiring fair in Dorchester with that of twenty or thirty years previously, Hardy observed:

'Formerly they came in smock-frocks and gaiters, the shepherds with their crooks, the carters with a zone of whipcord round their hats, thatchers with a straw tucked into the brim, and so on...but the genuine white smock-frock of Russia duck and the whitey-brown one of drabbet, are rarely seen now afield, except on the shoulders of old men.'

Hardy accounted for these changes by the 'rage for cloth clothes which possesses the labourers of today'. Like many of his

Detail of a Paisley shawl which reputedly belonged to Thomas Hardy's mother. This must have been a highly-prized and luxurious accessory.

contemporaries, Hardy's views on the changes he saw around him were, to some extent, coloured by feelings of regret and nostalgia. However, probably what Hardy was referring to was the growing availability of urban styles of dress, in particular, ready-made suits, many of which were of poor quality but were considered to be more fashionable than the traditional smock-frock.

Like men's clothing, fashions were changing for women too. The reasons for this are complex, but the decline of field work as a 'respectable' occupation meant that traditional, protective clothing and headgear were becoming redundant. Coupled with this was the fact that growing numbers of women and young girls were going into service, a form of employment which gave them access to ideas about new fashions, which they then took back with them to their villages when they were on holiday. Once again, Hardy's views on these changes were disparaging:

'. . . That peculiarity of the English urban poor . . . – their preference for the cast-off clothes of a richer class to a special attire of their own – has, in

fact, reached the Dorset farm folk. Like the men, the women are, pictorially, less interesting than they used to be. Instead of the wing bonnet like the tilt of a waggon, cotton gown, bright-hued neckerchief, and strong, flat boots and shoes, they (the younger ones at least) wear shabby millinery bonnets and hats with beads and feathers, 'material' dresses, and boot-heels almost as foolishly shaped as those of ladies of highest education.'

Although it is extremely rare to find one of the traditional cotton gowns Hardy refers to in this passage (the bodice of one survives at the Gallery of Costume, Manchester Art Gallery, a number of 'wing bonnets' were kept and have survived down to the present day. More usually described as sun-bonnets, both the Dorset County Museum and Sherborne Museum have an interesting variety of these garments in their respective collections. Usually made of plain or printed (usually checked or flowered) cotton and hand and machine-sewn, these bonnets were worn to shield the wearer's face and neck from the sun. Not only were sun-tans distinctly unfashionable in the nineteenth century, but working all day in the heat of the sun would have caused severe sunstroke without the head being protected. In order to give the sun-bonnets their distinctive shape, cotton cord was inserted into rows of stitched 'channels' and even thin strips of cane were sometimes used, so that the bonnet resembled the hood of a pram.

Although worn primarily for protection against the sun, these bonnets were also considered picturesque and they continued to appear in paintings of the late nineteenth century, even though they had gone out of general use by this time. Some were decorated with ruffles and bows of the same fabric as the bonnet itself, and, ironically, although Hardy lamented their passing and their replacement by modern fashions, it seems likely that the sun-bonnet originally evolved from fashionable headwear of the 1820s and 1830s. It is interesting to compare, for example, the similarity between the style of sun-bonnets and that of a fashionable bonnet in the Dorset County Museum of grey-beige silk worn in the 1830s. The

Dress of printed cotton, 1795-1805. The style is typical of the high-waisted gowns of the Napoleonic era. There is evidence that the garment belonged to a servant, grandmother of a farmer's wife at Wool.

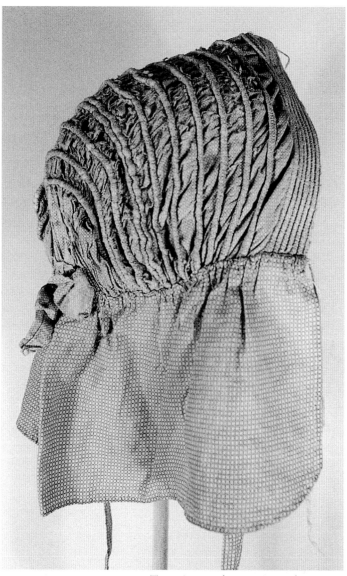

ABOVE AND OPPOSITE PAGE Two nineteenth century sun-bonnets.
The 'curtains' of the bonnet protected the face and neck of the
wearer from exposure to the sun when women worked outside for
much of the time. Both bonnets were bought by the author
at a local antique market in the 1980s for £1.50 each.

large number of sun-bonnets which survive reflect the individual tastes of their wearers - in terms of style, fabric and decoration. They also illustrate the fact that many women had to make the best of what was available to them. In *Tess of the d'Urbervilles*, Hardy describes the variety of clothing in the harvest scene:

'The women – or rather girls, for they were mostly young – wore drawn cotton bonnets with great flapping curtains to keep off the sun, and gloves to prevent their hands being wounded by the stubble. There was one wearing a pale pink jacket, another in a tight-sleeved gown, another in a petticoat as red as the arms of the reaping-machine; and others, older, in the brown-rough 'wropper' or over-all – the old-established and most appropriate dress of the field-woman, which the young ones were abandoning.'

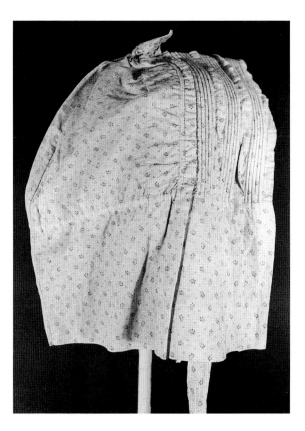

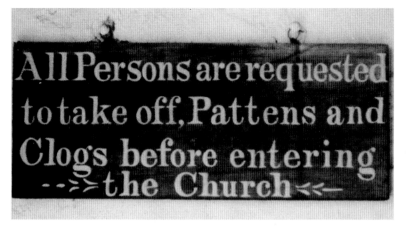

Notice in the church porch of St Andrews, Trent. Worn over shoes
for protection, pattens with their metal soles or 'irons' were not only
likely to be muddy and noisy, but also the hard soles could wear
down floors if worn indoors.

Some of the most expensive items of dress were boots and shoes,
and often the large outlay for these could only be afforded when there
was some extra income, usually at harvest-time. In this context, Tess's
loss of her walking boots after changing them for her 'pretty thin
ones of patent leather' and leaving the former at the side of the road
after her long walk to Emminster (Beaminster) in the hope of a
meeting with her parents-in-law, verges on tragedy. Boots and shoes
were highly prized and it is not surprising that country women wore
pattens (a sort of overshoe with a metal ring and base and leather
uppers with ties) over their shoes in order to protect their shoes
underneath. In *The Woodlanders* (1887), Marty South wears pattens
for her twelve-mile walk to Sherton Abbas (Sherborne) in order, she
says, to 'save' her boots. Hardy describes vividly the 'click, click' of
pattens being worn. Bearing in mind the noise made when wearing
pattens and the fact that the metal rings must have been potentially
damaging to floors (as well as muddy), it is interesting to find a notice
in the porch of the village church of St. Andrews in Trent which
reads: 'All Persons are requested to take off Pattens and Clogs before
entering the Church'. In 1823, Shaftesbury had 2 patten makers.

Nineteenth-century boot, possibly from Wimborne. Boots were expensive and repeatedly mended, hence the patch sewn over the heel area.

DRESSMAKERS, SHOEMAKERS AND CLOTHING CLUBS

While the majority of smock-frocks, sun-bonnets and other essential items of rural dress would have been sewn in the home, with children learning sewing skills from an early age, every village and town had its quota of dressmakers, milliners (in the larger villages and towns) and cobblers and shoemakers. Local mercers and drapers – in spite of their specialist names – tried to anticipate as many of their customers' needs as possible and the result was a huge array of goods all under one roof, from fabrics to dressmaking aids (haberdashery) and even accessories. In the larger villages and towns, however, shops were likely to be more specialist in nature, with Blandford in 1823 boasting the following: 8 boot and shoemakers; 2 glovers; 2 hatters; 8 linen drapers and manufacturers of shirt buttons; 6 tailors and drapers and no fewer than 9 milliners. Meanwhile, Dorchester had 9 boot and shoemakers; 2 hatters; 3 hosiers; 8 linen drapers; 5 straw hat makers and 7 tailors and drapers.

These lists hide a wealth of skills, and the numbers of outlets for fabrics and makers of the finished articles reflect the high demand for clothing. Crafts such as shoemaking were highly skilled and cobblers were valuable members of local society, ekeing out the life of already worn shoes or boots. Shaftesbury was well-known for its boot and shoemakers, with 18 listed in 1823, most of them located in Bell Street, Salisbury Street, High Street and the St. James area. Bere Regis in 1841 had 18 cobblers to a population of 1,394, which is hard to imagine now when walking through its quiet streets.

ABOVE A nineteenth-century hat discovered in the ceiling loft of a shop in Cornhill, Dorchester – perhaps a remnant of the stock of an earlier men's outfitters. The high crown is typical of the period, and was worn by all classes.
OPPOSITE PAGE Cobbler, Puddletown, in about 1899. The cobbler was an extremely important member of town and village society. As shoes were so expensive, the cobbler had to use his considerable skills and ingenuity to make them last as long as possible.

An 1862 notice by E. Steele of Dorchester announcing, 'his Milliners return from London, and that his Show Rooms for Millinery, Mantles, Straw Bonnets, Hats, etc, of the newest designs, will be ready for inspection.' Increasingly, provincial centres such as Dorchester made fashionable clothing available to its inhabitants.

Equally, dressmaking was an important business, with dressmakers competing for custom. In Bere Regis there were 4 dressmakers listed in 1841, although 10 years later, their number had risen to 16. As Barbara Kerr records in her book, *Bound to the Soil*, one particular Bere Regis dressmaker, Elizabeth Boswell, was extremely successful: an apprenticeship in her establishment was eagerly sought in the 1880s, although it involved working without pay from 9am to 8pm, with breaks for lunch and tea. Time off was allowed for choir practice providing it was made up on Saturday.

A fashionably dressed group in Lyme Regis in the 1870s. Up-to-date clothing styles began filtering down the social scale as more young women went into domestic service, bringing back ideas about the latest fashions from their employers to their home towns and villages.

Frequently, clothing (especially shoes or boots) could only be afforded when there was extra income brought into the household through harvest earnings, for example. Alfred Austin, the parliamentary commissioner charged with enquiring into the employment of women and children in agriculture in 1843 in Dorset commented on the fact that children – whether they were serving farm apprenticeships or not – were often prevented from attending church because, although those with apprenticeships are 'sufficiently clothed for their work, they sometimes have no better kind of clothing for the Sunday, and their masters are ashamed to let them appear at church in their ordinary dress of the week'. In the parish of Hilton, the story was the same: 'many children are also hindered in their attendance of school and church for want of decent clothes or shoes'.

Many of the shops which sold ready-made items of clothing also continued to offer a dressmaking service, as can be seen in this photo of Nun and Harlow, South Street, Dorchester, in about 1905.

For the poor, the local clothing club was perhaps the only means to obtaining suitable clothing. At Blandford, wrote Austin, 'any labouring family of good conduct' could belong to the clothing club by subscribing 1d., 2d., or 3d. per week, according to family size and circumstances:

'At the end of the year, these subscriptions are doubled by the donations of persons in a better position of life living in the neighbourhood. The subscribers are then entitled to purchase of the tradesmen appointed to supply the club, to the amount of their respective shares of the funds, any plain articles of dress or household linen.'

While Austin believed that, 'the effect of these clubs has been very great in increasing the linen and clothes of the labourers' families since their establishment', he admitted that the clergy 'are nearly always the main supporters and frequently the managers of the

A variety of hats (in particular straw boaters) were to be had from
William Evans, Dorchester, as can be seen in this photo, taken
before 1914. Striking window displays were frequently
the most effective means of advertising.

clothing clubs'. Worrying is the fact that it was also the clergy who decided whether the family was 'of good conduct' and who the 'tradesmen' would be to supply the club.

By the last decades of the nineteenth century, after the worst of the agricultural depression, wages gradually rose. More young women left their home villages in order to take up a position in service in the towns, their parents giving valuable custom to local dressmakers as great efforts were made to provide daughters leaving home with a new dress. When these girls returned home for their annual holiday, their small savings were often spent on having clothes made for their mothers and sisters.

Equally, by this time, cheaper ready-made clothes and shoes were increasingly available in the towns. Although the stigma of 'inferior quality' attached to these goods took many decades to evaporate, the 'modern' practice of buying our clothing 'off the peg' had definitely begun. The long-term result was the loss of many of the skills that had once been so prized and the continuing depopulation of the villages by those in search of more lucrative employment.

CRAFT REVIVALS

As an epilogue to this history of dress and textiles in Dorset, it seems fitting to describe some of the revivals of interest in needlework in the twentieth century. Much of this is due to individuals whose enthusiasm has captured the imagination of others, and without which these skills might otherwise have been lost. Perhaps the most important of these has been the revival of smock-making and buttony, although there have been other isolated cases of revivals, such as that of sun-bonnet making in the village of Bloxworth, which was introduced in 1913.

While smocks continued to be worn by older men who were less likely to change the dressing habits of a lifetime, they had, as we have seen, gone out of general fashion in the countryside by the late nineteenth century. However, the persistence of a perceived association between the design and embroidery of smocks and the individual, hand-crafted product may account for the adoption of smocks for wear by middle-class female followers (and their children) of the Arts and Crafts Movement. Furthermore, the frequent appearance of smocks in Kate Greenaway's illustrations of children in rural settings (seen, for example, in her hugely popular *Under the Window*, published in 1878) and the popularity of smocking on children's "Kate Greenaway dresses" sold by the costume department at Liberty's of London from the 1880s helped to take the smock out of the context in which it was originally worn and give it a renewed lease of life. One of the smocks at the Dorset County Museum is a young girl's smock from the late nineteenth or early twentieth century, and resembles in many respects these "Kate Greenaway dresses". It is decorated with lace and the level of technical skill displayed by the embroidery is very high.

In this context it is interesting to consider the revival of smock-making by the Bere Regis Arts and Crafts Association, of which the girl's smock is thought to be an example. The association was formed around 1905 by Sarah Lucy Bere, wife of the Rev. Montague Acland Bere, who was vicar of Bere Regis from 1905 to 1919, with the object of interesting local workers in the making of raffia baskets and traditional smocks. In particular, Mrs Bere admired the artistic qualities of smocks and it is probable that her interest was aroused in the first place by the smocks in the Dorset County Museum, of which her uncle, Captain J. E. Acland, had been curator. Collecting patterns from various sources and locations, the Bere Regis Arts and Crafts Association used to meet on regular days each week in a special room in the vicarage and there seems to have been about 15 or 20 regular workers. Both the Reverend and Mrs Bere left for war service in 1916, returning in 1919. Although a few individual workers continued to take orders after that date, either direct or through Mrs Bere, the association ceased as such.

The Rural History Centre at Reading University – probably the largest and most comprehensive collection of items relating to the history of the countryside in Great Britain – has some fine examples of Bere Regis smocks. A number of these are adult smocks, made from linen in different pastel shades and decorated with finely executed embroidery using coloured threads and fastened with Dorset buttons (mostly of the crosswheel type). Others are children's smocks, indistinguishable from their adult counterparts except in size.

From an interest in the embroidery on smocks, the development of a special interpretation of feather stitch (one of the most common embroidery stitches found on smocks) took place in the 1950s. Mrs Olivia Pass, then chairman of the Dorset Federation of Women's Institutes, evolved a form of embroidery which became known as "Dorset Feather Stitchery". Mrs Pass took the basic feather stitch and further embellished it with overwhipping in a self or contrasting colour. She also added a decorative braid, ric-rac, an idea taken from the aprons of Eastern Europe. In 1951 the work of Mrs Pass' original 80 students was put on sale at the Bath and West Agricultural Show.

No doubt there are hundreds of less well-known individuals who have been and are inspired by the rich heritage of Dorset's clothing and textile trades and who have been tempted to practise some of

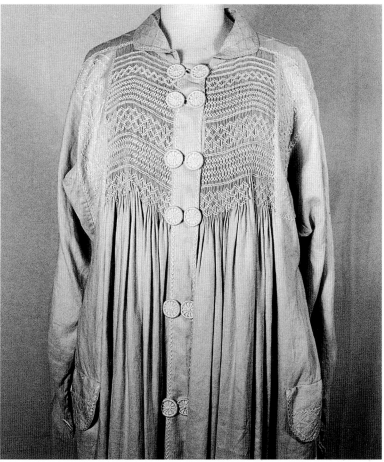

'Revival' smock probably made in the 1950s by the mother
of the donor, and decorated with traditionally-crafted
Dorset 'crosswheel' buttons.

these skills in their own homes. Significantly, Walford Mill in
Wimborne, once a fulling-mill for the Dorset woollen industry, now
hosts a number of exhibitions of the work of contemporary artists
and craftspeople, many of whom continue the traditions of the
county's rich history related to the production of dress and textiles.

FURTHER READING

Acland, John E., 'Dorset "Buttony"', *Proceedings of the Dorset Natural History and Archaeological Society*, Vol. 35, pp. 71-4, 1914

Baclawski, Karen, *The Guide to Historic Costume,* Batsford, 1995

Bettey, J.H., *Farming,* The Dovecote Press, 2000

Harper, Jean, *Sheep, Donkeys and the Pig: A Look into the Lives of the Glove-makers of Yeovil,* South Somerset Museum Service Publication, 2000

Kerr, Barbara, *Bound to the Soil: A Social History of Dorset,* John Baker Publishing, 1968

Mann, J. De L., *The Cloth Industry in the West of England, from* 1640-1880, Alan Sutton Publishing, 1987

Page, W., (eds.), *The Victoria County History of the Counties of England: A History of Dorset,* Vol II, 1908

Roberts, P.P., 'Richard Roberts, Flax-Spinner', *Proceedings of the Dorset Natural History and Archaeological Society*, Vol. 99, pp. 11-18, 1977

Stanier, P., *Mills,* The Dovecote Press, 2000

Symonds, H., 'The Silk Industry in Wessex', *Proceedings of the Dorset Natural History and Archaeological Society*, Vol. 37, pp. 66-93, 1916

Warren, F.C., 'Dorset Industries in the Past', *Proceedings of the Dorset Natural History and Archaeological Society*, Vol. 59, pp. 32-46, 1938

Worth, R., 'Thomas Hardy and Rural Dress', *Costume – The Journal of the Costume Society,* No. 29, pp. 55-67, 1995

ACKNOWLEDGEMENTS

I would like to thank Billie Brown and Valerie Dicker of Dorset County Museum for their considerable help with the illustrations. I am also grateful to Richard Brewer of Sherborne Museum; the staff of the Reference Department of Dorset County Library, Dorchester; Jo Draper for reading the text; Miss Joyce Gurr for providing digital images of four of the photographs; Mrs Thelma Johns of Old Button Shop Antiques, Lytchett Minster; Lyme Regis Museum; and Tracey Walker of Manchester Art Gallery, Gallery of Costume.

I am grateful to the following for allowing the inclusion of illustrations in their possession or for which they hold the copyright: Dorset County Museum; front and back covers, pages 2, 4, 6, 11, 12, 13, 16, 17, 18, 19 (both), 20, 24, 43, 45, 46, 49, 51, 54, 55 (top), 58, 67, 69, 70, 71; Miss Joyce Gurr 23, 47, 57, 59; Mrs Thelma Johns 40; Lyme Regis Museum 34; Sherborne Museum 26; Manchester Art Gallery 60.

The photographs on pages 20, 25, 31, 33, 38, 41, 42, 53, 55 (bottom), 56, 65, 66, 68, 75 are of objects in the collections of the Dorset County Museum, and I am grateful to Richard de Peyer for allowing them to be photographed. The bonnets on pages 62 and 63 are mine.

INDEX

The

DISCOVER DORSET

Series of Books

A series of paperback books providing informative illustrated
introductions to Dorset's history, culture and way of life.
The following titles have so far been published.

BRIDGES *David McFetrich and Jo Parsons*

CASTLES AND FORTS *Colin Pomeroy*

CRANBORNE CHASE *Desmond Hawkins*

CUSTOMS *Peter Robson*

DRESS AND TEXTILES *Rachel Worth*

FARMHOUSES AND COTTAGES *Michael Billett*

FARMING *J.H.Bettey* FOLLIES *Jonathan Holt*

FOSSILS *Richard Edmonds* GEOLOGY *Paul Ensom*

THE GEORGIANS *Jo Draper*

THE INDUSTRIAL PAST *Peter Stanier*

ISLE OF PURBECK *Paul Hyland*

LEGENDS *Jeremy Harte* LOST VILLAGES *Linda Viner*

MILLS *Peter Stanier* PORTLAND *Stuart Morris*

POTTERY *Penny Copland-Griffiths*

THE PREHISTORIC AGE *Bill Putnam*

RAILWAY STATIONS *Mike Oakley*

REGENCY, RIOT AND REFORM *Jo Draper*

THE ROMANS *Bill Putnam*

SAXONS AND VIKINGS *David Hinton*

SHIPWRECKS *Maureen Attwooll* STONE QUARRYING *Jo Thomas*

THE VICTORIANS *Jude James*

All the books about Dorset published by The Dovecote Press
are available in bookshops throughout the county,
or in case of difficulty direct from the publishers.
The Dovecote Press Ltd, Stanbridge,
Wimborne, Dorset BH21 4JD
Tel: 01258 840549   www.dovecotepress.com